GORILLAS

LIVING WILD

Published by Creative Education
P.O. Box 227, Mankato, Minnesota 56002
Creative Education is an imprint of The Creative Company
www.thecreativecompany.us

Design and production by Mary Herrmann
Art direction by Rita Marshall
Printed by Corporate Graphics in the United States of America

Photographs by Alamy (Black Star, Orokiet, Photos 12, United Archives GmbH, Ivan Vdovin), Corbis (Yann Arthus-Bertrand, Bettmann), Dreamstime (Martina Berg, Eric Gevaert, António Nunes, Poresh Petr, Glenda Powers, Tsuli, Ronald Van Der Beek, Patrick Van Maris), Getty Images (Francis Miller/Time & Life Pictures, Ian Nichols, Michael K. Nichols, Andrew Plumptre, Andy Rouse), iStockphoto (Diponkar Banerjee, Rob Friedman, Yves Grau, Guenter Guni, Jeff Gynane, Phil Hess, Eric Isseleé, Alan Lagadu, Warwick Lister-Kaye, Mamopictures M.G. Mooij, Russell McBride, Sharon Morris, William Murphy, Ricky Russ)

Library of Congress Cataloging-in-Publication Data
Gish, Melissa.
Gorillas / by Melissa Gish.
p. cm. — (Living wild)
Includes bibliographical references and index.
Summary: A look at gorillas, including their habitats, physical characteristics such as their large heads, behaviors, relationships with humans, and threatened status in the world today.
ISBN 978-1-58341-969-4
1. Gorilla—Juvenile literature. I. Title. II. Series.

QL737.P96G5537 2010
599.884—dc22   2009025170

CPSIA: 120109 PO1092
First Edition
9 8 7 6 5 4 3 2 1

CREATIVE EDUCATION

GORILLAS

Melissa Gish

On the western border of the African nation
of Rwanda, a thick rainforest covers Mount

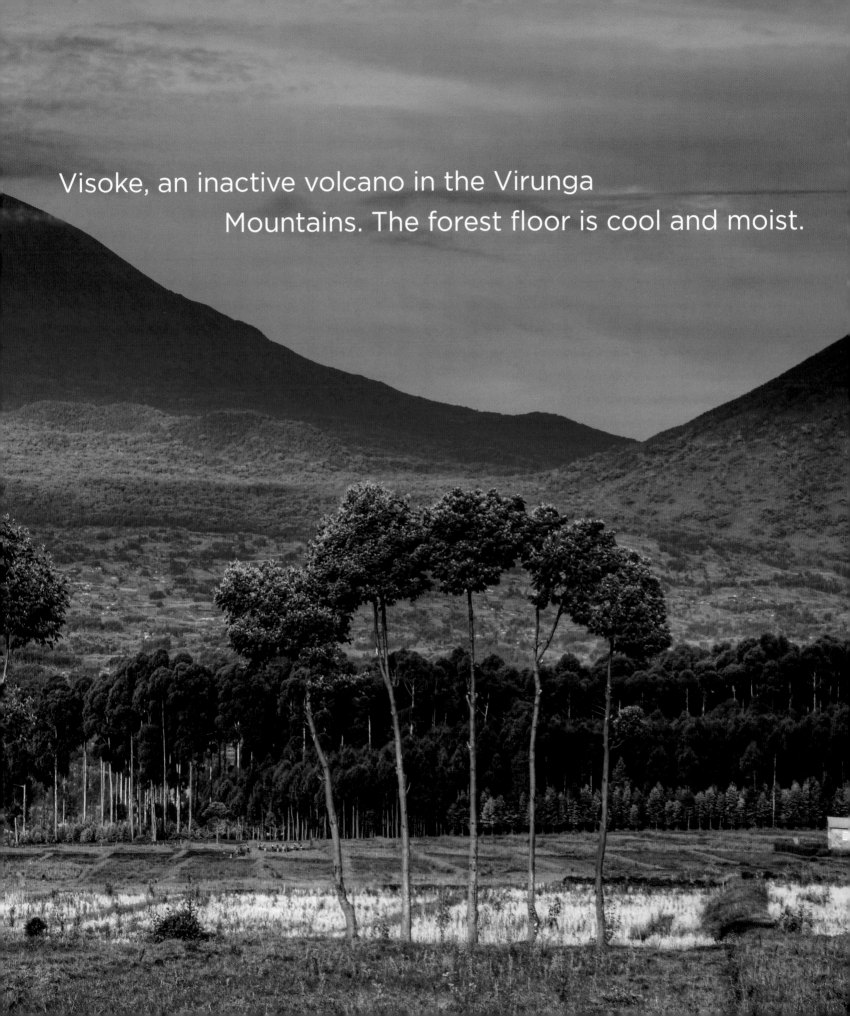

Visoke, an inactive volcano in the Virunga Mountains. The forest floor is cool and moist.

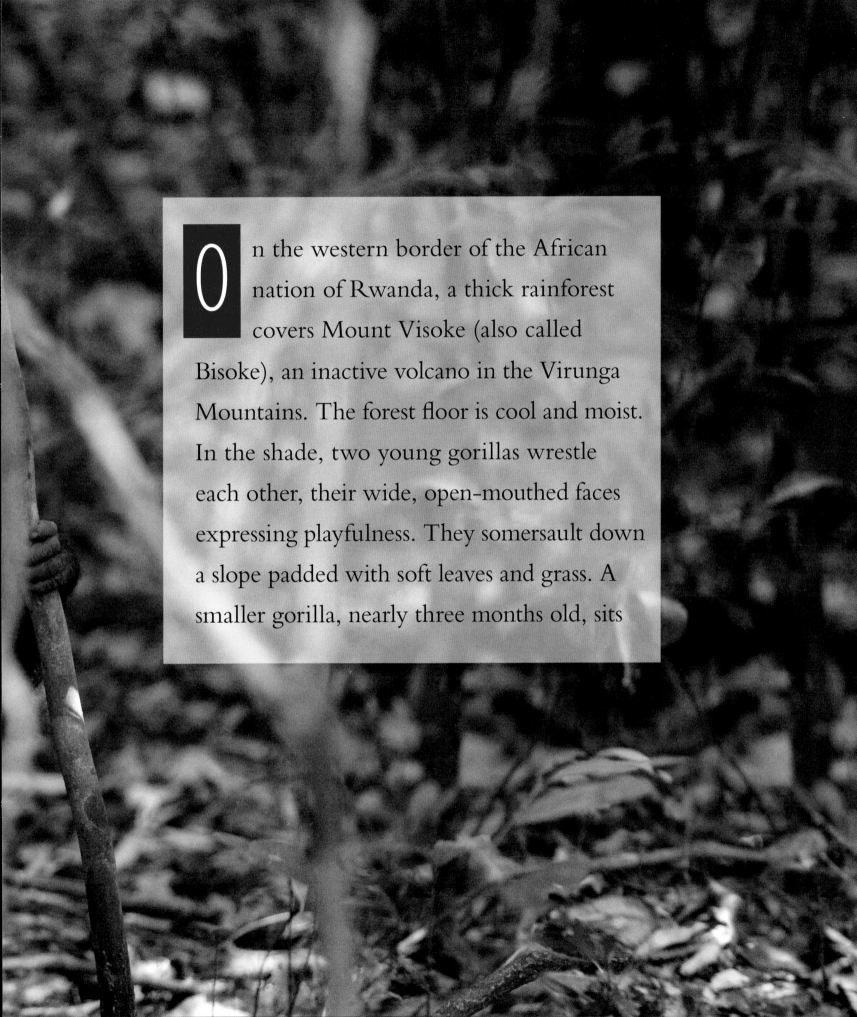

On the western border of the African nation of Rwanda, a thick rainforest covers Mount Visoke (also called Bisoke), an inactive volcano in the Virunga Mountains. The forest floor is cool and moist. In the shade, two young gorillas wrestle each other, their wide, open-mouthed faces expressing playfulness. They somersault down a slope padded with soft leaves and grass. A smaller gorilla, nearly three months old, sits

close to its mother, quietly nibbling tender leaves for the first time in its life. A fuzzy yellow caterpillar inches across a nearby branch, and the young gorilla cautiously rubs a knuckle on it. For gorillas, life in the rainforest is calm and peaceful. The sounds of birds calling and insects buzzing are constant—a part of life that goes unnoticed. A breeze rustles the leaves in the treetops as the young gorillas tire of their play and join their mothers for an afternoon nap.

■ **Western Lowland Gorilla**
west-central Africa west of the Congo River

■ **Eastern Lowland Gorilla**
central Africa east of the Congo River

■ **Cross River Gorilla**
west-central Africa between Nigeria and Cameroon

■ **Mountain Gorilla**
Uganda, Rwanda, and the Democratic Republic of the Congo

The four subspecies of gorilla recognized today all stem from two species, the western and eastern gorillas, and all are native to western and central Africa. The colored dots represent some common territories of gorillas that continue to live in the wild.

RAINFOREST RULERS

Gorillas are found in rainforests only on the continent of Africa. Around 500 B.C., Hanno the Navigator traveled from the North African city of Carthage, through the Mediterranean Sea, and around the west coast of Africa. He named the large, furry creatures he encountered there *gorillai*, a Greek word translated to mean "wild, hairy people."

Gorillas are apes and belong to the group of **mammals** called **primates**. As apes, gorillas are most closely related to chimpanzees and orangutans. Apes are sometimes confused with monkeys, but the two animals are very different from one another. Apes are tailless and have flat noses, while monkeys have tails and snouts. Additionally, apes have much larger brains and are more intelligent than monkeys.

Gorillas are covered with black hair except on their faces and on the palms of their hands and feet. Males average 5 to 6 feet (1.5–1.8 m) tall and weigh up to 500 pounds (227 kg). When they spread their arms, adult males can have an arm span of about eight feet (2.4 m). Females are generally smaller than males. They average just under 5 feet (1.5 m) tall and weigh 155 to 200 pounds (70–90 kg).

Gorillas' brains have a great capacity for memory, emotion, creativity, and language.

Gorillas have individual finger-prints just like humans, and they have unique nose prints that also can be used to identify individuals.

Unlike its darker-colored eastern cousin, the adult western lowland gorilla tends to be brown or grayish with a reddish forehead.

When males reach about 12 years of age, white hair covers their backs and shoulders, and they develop sharp canine teeth. These gorillas are known as silverbacks. Mature males from 8 to 11 years old are called blackbacks.

Male gorillas have especially powerful jaws, which is evidenced by the ridge of bone that protrudes across the top of their skulls. This bone is called a sagittal crest, and it serves as the connecting point for one of the main chewing muscles. Gorillas have bulky bodies with powerful limbs. They can stand upright, but they walk on their hind feet and the knuckles of their hands. This is called knuckle-walking, and chimpanzees and gorillas are the only primates to move this way. A gorilla's arms are longer than its legs, and its arm muscles are stronger than its leg muscles because its arms must support the enormous weight of its **torso** and head.

Gorillas are related to humans, who share almost 98 percent of their **DNA** with the apes, and like humans and other apes, gorillas have four fingers and a thumb on each hand and five toes on each foot. Their fingers and thumbs give them a strong grip and the ability to hold and manipulate objects with **dexterity**. They have fingernails

In 2002, the Wildlife Conservation Society discovered a new population of western lowland gorillas in the Republic of the Congo.

To avoid suffering from ticks and insects, gorillas spend many hours grooming themselves and their offspring.

and toenails instead of claws, which they keep trimmed by biting them. Because adult male gorillas are too heavy to climb many of the trees in their habitats, only smaller gorillas may be seen swinging through trees as they browse for food.

Gorillas sit upright when they eat, sometimes even crossing their legs like humans do. Gorillas are herbivores, meaning they get all of their nutrition from plants. Their diet consists of different plants, fruits, flowers, and bark that vary by region. In eating these foods, gorillas may consume insects, but they do not actively seek them as a food source. Adult gorillas can eat up to 60 pounds (27 kg) of food each day.

Gorillas rarely drink water. They get all the moisture they need from their food. Favorite foods include bamboo, wild celery, and thistles. Because they consume a great deal of plant matter every day, gorillas have adopted the efficient technique of folding up stacks of food into a kind of sandwich, which they then bite and shred with their sharp teeth. Researchers have also observed gorillas tearing off the tasty part of a plant or scooping out the inside of a fruit and leaving the leftovers in a neat pile.

To digest all of this food, gorillas have an extra-large and thick small intestine, which explains why gorillas have large bellies that extend past their chests. They also have a slow **metabolism**, and because digestion takes energy, gorillas sleep whenever they are not eating. They sleep 13 to 15 hours a night, doze after breakfast, nap for 2 or 3 hours after lunch, and then build a nest and go to sleep after supper.

While all gorillas share a similar appearance and behaviors, there are two distinct species of gorilla—western

Born at Ohio's Columbus Zoo in 1956, Colo was the first gorilla born in captivity and, as of 2009, was the oldest gorilla in captivity.

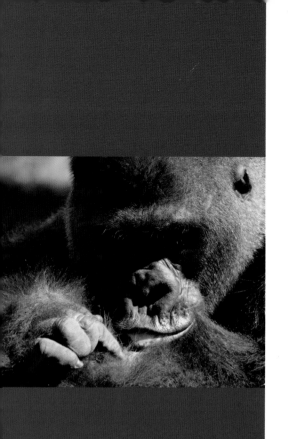

Gorillas establish and reinforce social bonds by grooming, combing through each other's hair with fingers and teeth to remove dirt and insects.

and eastern—which are divided into four subspecies. The Cross River gorilla (*Gorilla gorilla diehli*) and the western lowland gorilla (*Gorilla gorilla gorilla*) are subspecies of the western gorilla. The eastern lowland gorilla (*Gorilla beringei graueri*) and the mountain gorilla (*Gorilla beringei beringei*) are subspecies of the eastern gorilla.

A small number of Cross River gorillas live in the mountainous forests along the Nigeria–Cameroon border. Western lowland gorillas are found in a number of west-central African nations, including Cameroon, Gabon, and the Republic of the Congo (on the western side of the Congo River). These two gorilla subspecies are the most endangered of all African apes and appear on the Red List of Threatened Species that is published annually by the International Union for Conservation of Nature (IUCN).

The eastern lowland gorilla, found only in the forests of the eastern Democratic Republic of the Congo (on the eastern side of the Congo River), has longer teeth and a larger upper body than the two types of western gorillas; it also has darker hair. The mountain gorilla, the largest primate in the world, lives in fragmented areas of high mountain forests in Uganda, Rwanda, and the Democratic

Republic of the Congo. These gorillas have a unique appearance, with a higher and more pointed head and a wider nose gap than other types of gorillas. Their longer hair and additional body fat make mountain gorillas suited to their habitat, where temperatures can drop below freezing.

Recently, there has been debate over the definition of a possible third subspecies of eastern gorilla. While the **genetics** of Bwindi gorillas and other mountain gorillas are identical, the Bwindi is slightly smaller and lives at lower elevations than other mountain gorillas, leading some researchers to consider the Bwindi gorilla its own subspecies.

Protected by international law, the Bwindi Impenetrable National Park is a safe haven for mountain gorillas.

Baby gorillas develop such skills as crawling, walking, and lifting things twice as fast as human babies.

LIVING IN PEACE

Gorillas live in family groups, called troops, of about 5 to 30 members. Troops are organized by a ranking system called a hierarchy. A troop is led by a mature silverback whose responsibilities include defending the troop from other silverbacks who might want to take over, protecting young and weak members from predators such as leopards, and maintaining peace within the troop. Next in rank are the blackbacks, who assist the silverback in defending the troop. Females and their offspring under the age of seven are below the blackbacks, and females without offspring have the lowest status in the troop. When a troop moves through the forest, the silverback leads, and the other troop members follow in single file, according to their status.

Every member of the troop knows his or her place, and very little conflict occurs among members. Similar to human communication, gorillas use facial and body gestures and vocalizations to express meaning, make requests, and give commands. Whenever the silverback commands an action, the troop, trusting its leader's instincts, obeys without hesitation. The silverback communicates to his troop when they should eat, rest, travel, and sleep. When a silverback

Researchers have observed that gorillas do not eat all of the vegetation on trees and plants, allowing these food sources to continue growing.

When gorillas are calm and at rest (about 10 hours out of every day), they may make belch vocalizations.

turns to face a particular direction, opening his mouth wide to display his sharp teeth, he is saying to his troop, "Follow me." When a silverback perceives a sudden threat, he may emit a loud, screeching roar. This signal sends the troop scattering to take cover.

Gorillas use a variety of vocalizations. Hooting is used to communicate over long distances and help gorillas find each other when they have become separated from their troop. A silverback may also hoot at members of a rival troop. The sound means, "Stay away from my troop." A question bark is a series of three barks in a high-low-

high pattern. It expresses, "I can hear you, but I can't see you. Where are you?" Rumbling is a sound that gorillas make to tell others that they have found a good food source. Sounds categorized as belch vocalizations include humming, moaning, and soft grunting. These sounds indicate that a gorilla is calm and content.

Emotions such as sadness, joy, fear, and confusion can be easily interpreted by observing a gorilla's face. An angry gorilla will purse its lips, lower its eyebrows, and glare. It may also beat its chest with one or two open hands and throw sticks. An open mouth with raised

Gorillas have the same number of hairs per square inch (6.5 sq cm) on their bodies as humans—gorillas' hairs are just darker, thicker, and longer.

eyebrows, called a grimace, indicates fear. Gorillas can even smile to express happiness, and they laugh when they are tickled by one another. A gorilla play-face, characterized by a mouth wide open but not showing the teeth, is displayed when gorillas are only pretending to be aggressive toward one another.

The only predators that gorillas regularly encounter are leopards and humans. Leopards prey on sick, old, and infant gorillas. These big cats usually attack sleeping gorillas, because during the day, a silverback is ever watchful. With one swing of his arm, a silverback can break a leopard's back or crush its ribs. But gorillas are no match for humans with weapons and traps. Humans have hunted gorillas for generations and have, in fact, pushed gorillas to the brink of **extinction**.

People once thought gorillas were fierce and dangerous animals. Now it is known that gorillas are naturally some of the shyest and gentlest creatures on Earth. A silverback protects his troop by threatening, not fighting. Through displays of aggression such as standing and beating his chest—a clear alarm signal—and throwing sticks and dirt at an intruder, he shows his ability to protect his troop.

Young males imitate adults by beating their chests with open cupped hands to indicate excitement or aggression.

Gorillas are born toothless and develop "baby teeth," which fall out and are replaced by adult teeth—just like humans.

He may charge at the intruder but usually stops short of a fight. Only when the troop is seriously threatened will a silverback bite an intruder or beat it with his fists. Gorillas will not leave their wounded behind, and they defend their young fiercely.

Gorillas may live for 30 to 50 years. They reach maturity between the ages of 10 and 13. Females begin mating around age 10, typically giving birth once every 3 to 4 years. Females are allowed to breed only with the silverback in their troop. When blackbacks reach full maturity and begin to grow silver hair, they leave their family troops and gather their own troops of unrelated females. Gorillas will not mate with siblings or with unrelated gorillas they have grown up with, whom they consider stepsiblings.

Baby gorillas develop inside their mothers for eight and a half months before being born. This is just two weeks shorter than normal human **gestation**. A newborn gorilla weighs about four and a half pounds (2 kg). At first, the mother must hold the infant to her chest so it can feed on the milk she produces, but soon it grows strong enough to grip the hair of its mother's chest by itself. Later, it will

Gorillas can contract certain diseases from water sources polluted by humans.

Gorillas avoid deep water because they cannot swim, but they have been known to use sticks to check the depth of pools before wading across.

ride on her back as she moves through the forest. It will do this for the first year of its life and is able to clutch her hair with both its hands and feet, even while sleeping.

During this first year, a baby gorilla develops quickly. At around six weeks of age, it gets its first teeth. When it is 10 weeks old, it walks on all fours and begins to eat leaves and fruits. Two months later, it can climb trees, fearlessly exploring its surroundings and playing with other baby gorillas. It will never stray far from its mother, though, and will continue to nurse from her until it is about three years old.

All members of the troop—even the dominant silverback—participate in the nurturing of baby gorillas. Immature females learn how to carry and groom babies by watching the more experienced females. Adults play with babies, swinging them by their arms and legs, and gently wrestling with them, to help them build their muscles. Babies play with one another as well. They wrestle and play-fight, chase each other up and down trees, and somersault down hills. Such playful activities help young gorillas grow strong, learn how to get along with others in the troop, and practice finding food.

Gorillas rub noses and chins to greet each other, and they embrace each other to offer reassurance.

The 1933 film King Kong gave many people outside Africa an early—yet largely inaccurate—image of gorillas.

GORILLA POWER

Traditional gorilla masks are still carved out of wood by many people in the West African country of Ghana.

Whenever gorilla and human paths have crossed, humans have had varying reactions, from fear and hatred to respect and admiration. In gorillas' African habitats, some people consider them to be symbols of unlimited strength, while others believe they are evil. In many places, traditional legends about gorillas persist. The Bantu natives of Uganda believe that even saying "gorilla" in their language brings bad luck, but in Rwanda, the gorilla is the respected **totem** of the Twa tribe, who were the first inhabitants of the country, and it is forbidden to harm gorillas.

In northern Gabon, the Fang people carve small wooden statues, called fetishes, of human figures that feature the sagittal crest of a silverback gorilla, showing their belief in a spiritual connection between humans and gorillas. The Bamileke people native to Cameroon carve a special wooden mask with a gorilla's sagittal crest and teeth that only the tribal chief can wear. The people believe the mask gives the chief the power of the great apes.

Gorillas became part of many Africans' daily rituals as well. Drinking from gorilla skulls was thought to make

Gorillas have lost hands and feet in illegal wire snares that hunters set up to catch anything from rabbit-like hyraxes to water buffalo.

male children strong and fearless. Rubbing a person's back with stuffed gorilla hands was believed to transfer the gorilla's power into the person's body. The teeth of silverback gorillas would be worn on a necklace to give the wearer strength. And, according to one tribe in northwestern Cameroon, the Chamba, a new chief is **initiated** by eating a gorilla brain. This particular ritual is still performed today, but as gorilla populations in Africa remain low due to continued hunting and habitat loss, few people continue to include gorilla body parts in their rituals. Wealthy trophy collectors around the world, however, will pay great sums of money to **poachers** for gorilla heads, hands, and feet.

Gorilla symbols of strength and power extend far beyond the boundaries of Africa. Since 1980, a costumed gorilla has served as the mascot of the National Basketball Association's Phoenix Suns in Phoenix, Arizona. Today, the sports team also features a pair of inflatable gorillas, Hairy and Hairyson. At the college level, Pittsburg State University in Kansas is the only school in the United States with a gorilla mascot. Gus the Gorilla has helped inspire school spirit since the 1920s.

THE APE, THE MONKEY, AND BABOON

The ape, the monkey and baboon did meet,
And breaking of their fast in Friday street,
Two of them swore together solemnly
In their three natures was a sympathy.

Nay, quoth baboon,
I do deny that strain:
I have more knavery in me
than you twain.

Why, quoth the ape, I have a horse at will
In Paris Garden for to ride on still,
And there show tricks. Tush, quoth the monkey,
For better tricks in great men's houses lie.

Tush, quoth baboon,
when men do know I come,
For sport from city, country
they will run.

by Thomas Weelkes (1576–1623)

In Walt Disney Pictures'
Tarzan, *the young jungle*
boy learns life's lessons
from a loving gorilla family.

Because some people have long viewed gorillas as fierce and frightening, it is no surprise that fictional gorillas have often been portrayed in this light. Gorilla Grodd is a comic book supervillain who has tormented heroes such as The Flash and members of the Justice League since 1959. In an episode of the popular children's show *SpongeBob SquarePants*, two characters were attacked by a gorilla; and a gorilla criminal named Silver caused problems for the Teenage Mutant Ninja Turtles on the late 1990s TV show, *Ninja Turtles: The Next Mutation*. On the other hand, the animated gorilla Donkey Kong is a popular video game hero. Originally created in Japan in 1981, Donkey Kong went from having a supporting role in a simple arcade game into becoming a full-fledged character in 1994's Game Boy version of *Donkey Kong* and Super Nintendo Entertainment System's *Donkey Kong Country*.

In 1963, French novelist Pierre Boulle introduced the world to *The Planet of the Apes*, a science fiction story that takes place hundreds of years in the future when an astronaut discovers walking, talking apes—chimpanzees, orangutans, and gorillas—ruling a distant planet, while humans are kept as slaves and pets. The book spawned five

major films from 1968 to 1973, two television series that
aired from 1974 to 1976, and numerous books, comics, and
video games. More recently, filmmaker Tim Burton made
a new version of *The Planet of the Apes* in 2001.

   In 1914, the book *Tarzan of the Apes*, by American
author Edgar Rice Burroughs, was published and
introduced an orphan named Tarzan who is raised by
a troop of great apes. Numerous films, books, comics,
and television shows have been produced over the years,
showcasing Tarzan's complicated relationships with his ape
family and human society. In 1999, Walt Disney Pictures
released an animated film, *Tarzan*, which introduced the
lovable gorilla characters Kala, Kerchak, and Terk.

In Planet of the Apes, *gorillas'
relatives, the chimpanzees, are
intellectuals and scientists, while
humans are slaves.*

Gorillas will mourn the death of a troop member and bury it by covering the body with leaves.

Gorillas cry when they are sad or in pain; they do not cry tears, but they make sounds resembling those that humans make when crying.

Certainly one of the most famous fictional gorillas is King Kong, who was created by American filmmaker Merian C. Cooper and first appeared in a movie in 1933. The 50-foot-tall (15 m) gorilla lives with dinosaurs on the remote Skull Island, set in the Indian Ocean, and is captured by filmmakers who take him to New York City to put him on display. But Kong breaks free and climbs the Empire State Building, taking with him a beautiful woman whom he loves. In reality, Kong was a miniature puppet that stood only 18 inches (46 cm) tall. The film's special effects were remarkable for the time.

King Kong was followed by many sequels over the decades, and it was remade in 2005 by New Zealand director Peter Jackson. A scientific understanding of gorilla intelligence and greater attention to gorillas' true physical characteristics led to a change in the way King Kong was portrayed. Jackson's digitally animated Kong was shown as an expressive, emotional, and bright creature. For its remarkably lifelike portrayal of the gorilla—who is only 24 feet tall (7 m) according to this version—Skull Island, and 1930s New York City, Jackson's film won Academy Awards for visual effects, sound editing, and sound mixing.

Another creation of Merian C. Cooper's imagination was the character Mighty Joe Young. This gorilla began its rampage through Hollywood in 1949. Walt Disney Pictures remade the film in 1998, giving Joe a personality much more like that of a real gorilla—shy but curious and very intelligent. These are the main characteristics of gorillas that are expressed in the 1988 film *Gorillas in the Mist*. The movie is based on the 1983 book written by Dian Fossey, a **zoologist** who lived with mountain gorillas in the rainforests of Rwanda, studying them and revealing her astounding findings to the world.

To better monitor individual gorillas, Dian Fossey practiced the Rwandan tradition of naming them as newborns.

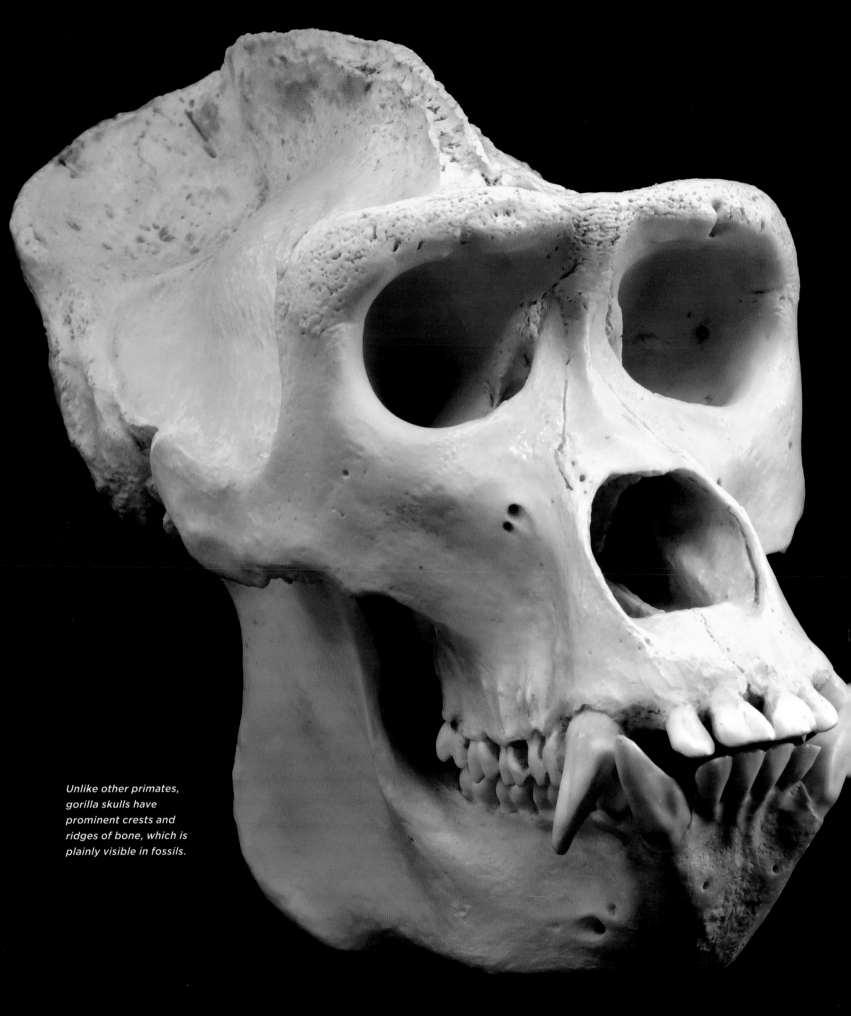

Unlike other primates, gorilla skulls have prominent crests and ridges of bone, which is plainly visible in fossils.

LEARNING FROM GORILLAS

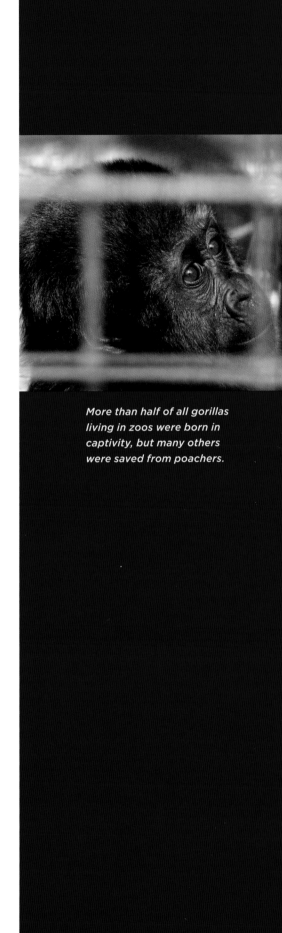

H umans did not **evolve** from apes, but many scientists believe that gorillas, chimpanzees, and humans all came from a common ancestor that existed in Africa and southern Asia about 15 million years ago. Gorilla ancestors **diverged** from the line of shared chimpanzee and human ancestry about 12 million years ago, while chimpanzees did not split from humans until 5 to 8 million years ago. The oldest gorilla fossils, the teeth of a 10-million-year-old species called *Chororapithecus abyssinicus*, were found in Ethiopia in 2007 by a team of Japanese and Ethiopian **paleoanthropologists**. The fossil remains of *Gigantopithecus*, a gorilla ancestor that lived about one million years ago, have been found in China. This creature was much larger than today's gorillas.

According to accounts by early 20th-century explorers and researchers, gorillas were once abundant across central Africa. In the last 50 years, however, gorilla populations have seriously declined. Hunting to support the **bushmeat** trade is a major culprit, as the nations where gorillas live are poor, and many people are desperate for food. Capturing baby primates for the illegal pet trade is

A gorilla rarely drinks water, but when it does, it drenches the back of its hand and then slurps the water collected in the hair.

another problem, and **deforestation** of rainforest habitat to make farmland disrupts many primate groups, leading to their demise. Researchers predict that if the hunting, capturing, and **displacing** of apes and monkeys does not stop, nearly 20 percent of the world's primate species—including perhaps gorillas—will be extinct by 2020.

Current research suggests that 35,000 to 95,000 western lowland gorillas and up to 5,000 eastern lowland gorillas now survive in the wild. Most captive gorillas are western lowland gorillas, and about 550 of that species live in zoos; fewer than 25 eastern lowland gorillas live in zoos. Only about 700 mountain gorillas and 250 to 300 Cross River gorillas still exist—and all are in the wild.

Major gorilla research projects began in the 1950s. German-American biologist George Schaller was the first to study gorillas in their native habitat. In 1959, Schaller traveled to Africa and lived with gorillas in the rainforest around the Virunga volcanoes. He published a book on mountain gorillas in 1963 that completely changed the public's view of gorillas and encouraged others to follow in his footsteps.

In 1967, Dian Fossey did just that. She founded the Karisoke Research Center in Rwanda, where she lived with mountain gorillas for 18 years, eventually being treated almost as a member of their troop. They touched her, let her play with their young, and napped with her. Her favorite gorilla was named Digit, and she watched him grow from an infant to an adult. When Digit was killed by poachers in 1978, Fossey was devastated.

Fossey told Digit's story to *National Geographic* magazine, and people responded by sending money to Fossey to help the gorillas. The funding enabled her to establish the Digit Fund and to take on the poachers in Rwanda, arming forest rangers with guns and ordering them to shoot poachers. In 1985, Fossey was murdered, possibly by someone who wanted to stop her work against poaching. But her death only prompted people around the world to create and fund more gorilla research and conservation programs.

In 1992, the U.S. branch of the Digit Fund was renamed the Dian Fossey Gorilla Fund International. Among its many projects, the organization supports Fossey's Karisoke Research Center, which is headquartered in Musanze, Rwanda, near Volcanoes National Park. The center employs numerous scientists and researchers, as well as 35 gorilla trackers and armed

Mountain gorillas are so reclusive that the species was not even known to science until 1902.

A female mountain gorilla may see only two to six of her offspring survive to maturity.

Every night, gorillas build simple sleeping nests of branches in trees or on the ground; they rarely use the same nest more than once.

forest rangers. The trackers and rangers patrol the park for poachers, and they destroy the deadly traps that are set for gorillas and other animals, such as leopards and antelope, which are killed for their skins and meat. The scientists at Karisoke study the health, habitat, social behaviors, population shifts, and genetics of gorillas.

African national governments have established a number of protected areas for gorillas, though human activity often confines the gorillas to very small areas or deters them from entering certain places altogether. Gorillas are legally protected in Uganda's Mgahinga Gorilla National Park, the Virunga National Park in the Democratic Republic of the Congo, and Volcanoes National Park in Rwanda. Parts of these three parks constitute the Virunga Conservation Area, a 167.6-square-mile (434 sq km) refuge for mountain gorillas.

One important type of gorilla research conducted by the Gorilla Foundation involves communication and language. The Gorilla Foundation was formed in 1976 by Americans Penny Patterson, a professor of psychology, and Ron Cohn, a biologist, who raised a gorilla named Koko from infancy and taught her to communicate using American

Many mountain gorillas live in the shadows of Nyiragongo, a volcano that has erupted more than 30 times since 1882.

Sign Language. The ongoing interspecies communication research is called Project Koko, and the almost 40-year-old Koko is still part of Patterson and Cohn's family.

Koko is well known around the world, as was her partner, Michael, who also communicated by signing. Patterson's 1987 book *Koko's Kitten* tells the story of Koko's special relationship with her pet kitten, whom she named "All Ball" because it was tailless. Based upon the success it experienced with Koko and Michael, the Gorilla Foundation has continued to raise money for research, education, and conservation efforts. It has also funded and constructed the Maui Ape Preserve in Hawaii, the first gorilla sanctuary outside of Africa and Koko's eventual new home.

Far from the African rainforests, in Chicago, Illinois, the Lincoln Park Zoo is the only place in the world that conducts research on both chimpanzee and gorilla **cognition** by using touch-screen computers. The gorillas are taught to touch numbers in specific sequences to get treats. One gorilla, a female named Rollie, participates in the experiments even without being rewarded. The research being conducted by the Lester E. Fisher Center for the Study and Conservation of Apes is geared toward examining primate intellect and language in an effort to better understand how these abilities develop.

Despite many people's appreciation for gorillas and their valuable contributions to scientific and behavioral research, these animals are dangerously close to extinction. They struggle against the effects of disease and human influence from poaching, civil war, and poverty. Large-scale conservation efforts are critical to saving these remarkable animals for future generations to learn from and admire.

Koko the gorilla has a vocabulary of more than 1,000 signs, and she even creates her own words, such as signing "finger bracelet" to mean "ring."

ANIMAL TALE: WHY GORILLAS DO NOTHING ALL DAY

The Congo River, the world's second largest, flows along the eastern border of the Democratic Republic of the Congo. The river, as well as the gorillas that once made the river valley their home, figure prominently in this tale from the region.

One rainy season long ago, the mighty Congo River overflowed its banks, flooding the valley and threatening to drown all of the inhabitants of the forest. Animals ran quickly toward the hills, racing the floodwaters to reach higher ground, but many of them were too small, too old, or too weak. They needed help.

The gorillas, being compassionate but strong creatures, stayed behind to help others who could not make the journey on their own. The gorillas climbed into the trees with their unfortunate animal neighbors on their backs and carried them to safety. Then they returned to the river to look for anyone who might have been left behind.

Looking down into the rushing floodwaters, the gorillas saw the fish flapping their tails and leaping from the water. One of the gorillas shouted to another, "Look! The fish are drowning! See how they struggle in the water!"

"Yes," said another gorilla. "They have no legs to run to the hills. We should save them!" So the gorillas swung from branch to branch toward the river. They jumped into the water, swimming against the strong current. The fish flapped and leaped all around them, and the gorillas reached out and scooped up as many fish as they could. Then they climbed back into the trees and carried the fish to the high hills, where they laid the fish on the dry land.

This went on all night. The gorillas pulled the fish from the river and carried them to the hills. Finally, the gorillas, who were exhausted, drenched, and shivering, collapsed on the hillside beside a huge pile of fish. The next morning, as the sun began to peek above the treetops, the gorillas awoke to find all of the other animals standing around the pile of fish. "What have you done?" exclaimed a hippopotamus.

"The fish were struggling so pitifully," said one of the gorillas, "we had to save them from drowning." The gorillas gathered around the pile of fish, expecting them to awaken and be thankful. But the fish didn't move, and some flies began buzzing around them.

"Fish don't drown in the river," the hippopotamus explained to the gorillas. "They need the water to breathe. It is on dry land that they die."

"Oh, no," said one gorilla. "Indeed, what have we done?" All of the animals began to shake their heads and make *tsk tsk tsk* sounds at the gorillas. "We are very sorry," said another gorilla. "What should we do?"

"You should do nothing," said the hippopotamus, "ever again!" All of the animals agreed. "Nothing," said the leopard from atop a rock. "Nothing at all," the **Damara tern** called down from a tree branch. The gorillas were saddened by their mistake. "As you wish," they told their animal neighbors. "We will do nothing."

And for this reason, gorillas do not climb trees and swing from branch to branch. They do not swim in the river. And they do not catch fish. Gorillas do nothing all day but munch on leaves and rest in the shade of tall trees.

GLOSSARY

bushmeat – the meat of wild animals killed for food or for sale in tropical parts of the world such as Asia and Africa

cognition – the mental process of gaining understanding through experience, thought, and the senses

Damara tern – a black bird with webbed feet and a short beak that lives along African shorelines and feeds on small fish

deforestation – the clearing away of trees from a forest

dexterity – skill or agility in using the hands or body to perform tasks

displacing – being forced to leave one's home due to destruction or disaster

diverged – developed in a different direction

DNA – deoxyribonucleic acid; a substance found in every living thing that determines the species and individual characteristics of that thing

evolve – to gradually develop into a new form

extinction – the act or process of becoming extinct; coming to an end or dying out

genetics – relating to genes, the basic physical units of heredity

gestation – the period of time it takes a baby to develop inside its mother's womb

initiated – admitted into a group through a formal ceremony or ritual

mammals – warm-blooded animals that have a backbone and hair or fur, give birth to live young, and produce milk to feed their young

metabolism – the processes that keep a body alive, including making use of food for energy

paleoanthropologists – people who study extinct members of human ancestry

poachers – people who hunt protected species of wild animals, even though doing so is against the law

primates – mammals with large brains and gripping hands; lemurs, monkeys, apes, and humans are primates

torso – the trunk of the body (not including head, arms, or legs)

totem – an object, animal, or plant respected as a symbol of a tribe and often used in ceremonies and rituals

zoologist – a person who studies animals and their lives

SELECTED BIBLIOGRAPHY

Caldecott, Julian, and Lera Miles, eds. *World Atlas of Great Apes and their Conservation.* Berkeley: University of California Press, 2005.

The Gorilla Foundation. "Homepage." http://www.koko.org.

Hanson, Thor. *The Impenetrable Forest: My Gorilla Years in Uganda.* Warwick, N.Y.: 1500 Books LLC, 2008.

Mountain Gorilla Conservation Fund. "Homepage." http://www.saveagorilla.org.

Robbins, Martha M., Pascale Sicotte, and Kelly J. Stewart, eds. *Mountain Gorillas: Three Decades of Research at Karisoke.* Cambridge: Cambridge University Press, 2005.

Weber, Bill, and Amy Vedder. *In the Kingdom of the Gorillas: Fragile Species in a Dangerous Land.* New York: Simon & Schuster, 2002.

Gorillas are some of the most skilled problem solvers of all mammals—even able to get themselves out of tricky spots.

INDEX

_____